Sugar-Free Cookie Reci[pes]

A Yummy Bite to A Healthy Diet - Best Ideas for Sugar-Free Cookies

BY - Charlotte Long

License Page

Table of Contents

Introduction

Sugar-free cookies are often thought to be as dull, tasteless little things that you force down your throat in the name of the diet isn't it. Well, not anymore! Because here, I bring some of the easiest yet mind-blowing recipes for sugar-free cookies that will win your heart. These cookies are the answer to all your healthy snack problems. No compromise with taste, nor any compromise with health.

No matter if it's for yourself or to impress the ones you love, these sugar-free cookies are fit for all occasions. A healthy choice you won't regret! So just get set with your kitchen gears to spread the aroma of your baking magic all over the house. Happy baking!

1. Paleo Chocolate Chip Cookies

When it comes to cookies, the first option should always be the one with chocolate chips. So, paleo chocolate chip cookies are the first on our list to help you with your tasty diet plan. Sit with a glass of hot milk and these cookies and forget all your anxiety.

Ingredients:

- 1 large egg
- 1/2 tsp. baking soda
- 2 and 1/4 cups blanched almond flour
- Flaky sea salt, for serving
- 2/3 cup coconut sugar
- 1/2 tsp. sea salt
- 1 cup chopped dark chocolate
- 1/2 cup refined coconut oil
- 1 tsp. pure vanilla extract

Cooking Time - 80 minutes

Serving Size - 16 cookies

Instructions:

Combine the coconut sugar with the coconut oil till the mixture is smooth. Stir the vanilla extract along with the egg into the mixture and continue stirring till it is perfectly smooth.

Add the baking soda, salt, and almond flour to the wet mixture and combine till everything is mixed well. Stir the chopped dark chocolate as well. Place this mixture properly covered inside a refrigerator and chill for about an hour.

Remove from the refrigerator once you are prepared to bake. Get the oven ready by preheating it to 350 degrees F. Form about 12 cookies with the help of a cookie scoop and get ready on a baking sheet lined with parchment. Gently, use the back of the cookie scoop to press down. Dust flaky sea salt all over the cookie tops.

Place inside the oven and bake for about ten minutes till the cookies begin to turn light brown towards the edges. Serve or store however you wish.

2. Peanut Butter Chocolate Chip Cookies

Butter is a fatty food but is there a healthy alternative? Of course, peanut butter! When incorporated with this amazingly delicious recipe, this protein-rich yummy ingredient gives out some mouth-watering cookies.

Ingredients:

- 2/3 cup coconut sugar
- 1 and 1/2 tsp. vanilla extract, pure
- 1/2 cup creamy peanut butter
- 1 and 2/3 cups almond flour, blanched
- 1/2 tsp. baking soda
- 2/3 cups dark chocolate chunks
- 1/3 refined coconut oil
- 1 large egg
- 1/2 tsp. baking powder
- 1/2 tsp. sea salt
- 1/2 cup mini dark chocolate peanut butter cups (chopped)

Cooking Time - 20 minutes

Serving Size - 12

Instructions:

Combine the coconut sugar with the coconut oil in a large bowl and keep mixing till the mixture is fluffy and light. Stir in vanilla extract and peanut butter along with the egg. Blend till the mixture is smooth.

Combine the salt, baking soda, and baking powder with the flour and add this mixture to the peanut butter mix. Combine well till everything is blended well.

Toss the chopped peanut butter cups and chocolate chunks into the mixture. Cover the dough and refrigerate for about an hour. Remove from the refrigerator once you're ready to bake. Divide the dough into 12 balls.

Prepare the oven by preheating it to 350 degrees F. Place the cookie balls on a parchment-lined baking sheet and use the back of a spoon to press down gently. Bake for about 10-12 minutes till the cookies are golden brown by the edges.

Let the cookies cool down for five minutes or so. Serve or store as per your wish.

3. Gluten-Free Vegan Peppermint Cookies

If you are on a vegan diet along with your diabetic diet, here's one perfect variant made just for you. With the fresh flavor of peppermint melting in your mouth, these vegan cookies are all you need to satiate your midnight hunger.

Ingredients:

- 2/3 cup coconut sugar
- 1 tsp. pure vanilla extract
- 1/2 tsp. baking soda
- 2 and 1/4 cups blanched almond flour
- 1/4 cup crushed candy canes
- 1/2 cup refined coconut oil
- 3 ounces melted dark chocolate
- 1 large egg
- Crushed candy canes, for serving
- 1/2 tsp. peppermint extract
- 1/2 tsp. sea salt
- 1 cup chopped dark chocolate

Cooking Time -25 minutes

Serving Size - 16

Instructions:

Combine the coconut sugar with the coconut oil till the mixture is smooth. Stir in peppermint, vanilla, and egg; continue stirring till the mixture blends well.

Add the baking soda, salt, and almond flour to the wet mixture. Combine well while folding in the crushed candy canes and chopped chocolate. Refrigerate this mixture, covering it properly.

Prepare the oven by preheating it to 350 degrees F. Form about 16 cookies with the help of a cookie scoop and line the cookies on a baking sheet lined with parchment paper. Gently press down with the back of the cookie scoop.

Let the cookies bake till the edges get golden browned, about ten minutes later. Cool the cookies for a while after removing them from the oven. Add the finishing touch with a melted chocolate drizzle and sprinkle the candy canes.

Serve or store as you require.

4. Flourless Strawberry Chocolate Chip Cookies

A sweet and sour strawberry essence with little choco-chip delight in between; no wonder why this one is so popular among all. Maybe you should try and decide for yourself.

Ingredients:

- 1/2 cup coconut sugar
- 1 tsp. baking soda
- 1/2 cup dark chocolate chips
- 1 cup smooth cashew butter
- 1 egg
- 1 cup freeze-dried strawberries, ground to powder

Cooking Time - 20 minutes

Serving Size - 12

Instructions:

Get the oven ready by preheating it to 350 degrees F. Prepare the cookie dough by first whisking the coconut sugar, baking soda, cashew butter, strawberry powder, and egg together in a mixing bowl. Toss the chocolate chips into the mixture and stir till blended well.

Divide the cookie dough into 12 balls. Place these balls on a silicone mat-lined baking sheet. Gently press down the cookie balls onto the baking sheet and place them in the oven.

Bake for about 10 minutes till the cookies are golden brown and properly set. Remove them and let them cool for a while.

Serve or store in an airtight container, as you prefer.

5. Mocha Chocolate Chip Cookies

Cheese with chocolate now doesn't sound fun! Crispy crust with a smooth inside that melt over your tongue feels like heaven. This mocha chocolate chip cookie is going to leave a taste that makes you crave more.

Ingredients:

- 3/4 cup coconut sugar
- 1 tsp. vanilla extract
- 1 tbsp. instant espresso powder
- 1/2 tsp. salt
- 1/2 cup chopped dark chocolate
- 1/2 cup coconut oil
- 1 large egg
- 2 and 1/4 cups blanched almond flour
- 1 tbsp. cacao powder
- Flaky sea salt, for garnish
- 1/2 tsp. baking soda

Cooking Time - 20 minutes

Serving Size - 15

Instructions:

Whisk the coconut sugar with the coconut oil while adding vanilla and egg. Mix till the mixture is well blended. Stir in the cacao powder, almond flour, salt, baking soda, and espresso powder. Toss the chopped chocolate and fold it into the mixture.

Refrigerate the cookie dough, covering it well for about 1 hour. Meanwhile, get the oven ready by preheating it to 350 degrees F. Once ready for baking, form 15 cookies with the help of the cookie scoop. Place all of them on a baking sheet lined with parchment paper. Press down gently with the back of the cookie scoop.

Garnish with flaky sea salt by dusting it all over the cookies. Bake for about ten minutes and remove from the oven once the cookies are lightly browned towards the edges.

Serve immediately, or store for later.

6. Paleo and Soft Gingerbread Cookies

The most delicious Gingerbread cookies are refined sugar-free, dairy-free, gluten-free, and grain-free. Sweetness added by coconut sugar, these healthy cookies are a great choice for a holiday treat.

Ingredients:

- 1/2 cup coconut sugar
- 1/2 tsp. salt
- 1/2 cup coconut flour
- 1/3 cup almond butter
- 2 tbsp. virgin coconut oil
- 1/4 cup molasses
- 1 large egg
- 1 tsp. vanilla extract
- 1 tsp. ground ginger
- 1/2 tsp. baking soda
- 1 tsp. cinnamon
- 1/4 tsp. ground nutmeg

For Rolling the Dough:

- 1/4 tsp. ground ginger
- 1/4 tsp. cinnamon
- 1/3 cup coconut sugar

Cooking Time - 21 minutes

Serving Size - 12

Instructions:

Get the oven ready by preheating it to 350 degrees F and get the baking sheet lined with parchment paper. Prepare the dough by whisking the almond butter, coconut sugar, coconut oil, and molasses till the mixture is smooth. Stir in the vanilla and egg and continue mixing till they blend properly.

Add cinnamon, salt, coconut flour, ginger, baking soda, and nutmeg to the mixture. Fold well till all the ingredients and combine properly.

Prepare the mixture to roll the dough by combining the ground ginger, cinnamon, and coconut sugar in another bowl. Form cookies from the dough using a cookie scoop and then roll those cookies in the sugar mixture.

Line the cookies on the baking sheet and gently flatten them before placing them inside the oven. Bake for about 10-12 minutes and remove from the oven once the cookies are golden brown.

Take them out of the oven and allow them to cool. Serve warm or save for later in airtight containers.

7. Peanut Butter Oatmeal Raisin Cookies

Dry fruits add a magic touch to whichever food they go to. In these yummy peanut butter oatmeal cookies, you will feel that magic touch added by premium raisins. Moreover, the use of almond flour makes it a perfect option for people on a gluten-free diet.

Ingredients:

- 2/3 cup coconut sugar
- 1/2 tsp. baking powder
- 1/2 cup creamy peanut butter
- 3/4 cup rolled oats, gluten-free, old fashioned
- 1/2 tsp. kosher salt
- 1 cup raisins
- 1/2 cup coconut oil
- 1 tbsp. vanilla extract
- 1 egg
- 1 cup blanched almond flour
- 1/2 tsp. baking soda
- 1 tsp cinnamon
- Chocolate chips for garnish

Cooking Time - 27 minutes

Serving Size - 18

Instructions:

Beat the coconut sugar with the coconut oil in a big bowl. Stir in the vanilla extract, egg, and peanut butter; whisk till the contents are blended well.

Add the almond flour, baking soda, oats, baking powder, cinnamon, and salt into the mixture. Whisk well till all the ingredients mix. Toss the raisins and chocolate chips; fold them into the mixture. Cover and chill for about two hours till ready to bake.

Get the oven preheated to 350 degrees F. Divide the cookie dough into 18 rounded cookie balls. On a parchment-lined baking sheet, place the cookie balls and flatten gently. Place inside the oven and bake for about twelve minutes.

Remove from the oven once the cookies are golden brown. Let them cool down for a bit, and then serve warm.

8. Chocolate Chip Pumpkin Cookies

Who said pumpkins could only be the Halloween delight? We have tricks to bring this pumpkin delight for your everyday treat too. Loaded with the all-time favorite chocolate chips, these freshly baked cookies will remind us of the good old Halloween days.

Ingredients:

- 3/4 cup canned pumpkin puree
- 2 tsp. vanilla extract
- 1/2 tsp. nutmeg
- 1 tsp. baking powder
- 1/2 tsp. kosher salt
- 1/3 cup and 1 tbsp. coconut flour
- 1/2 cup coconut oil
- 1 cup dark chocolate chunks
- 3/4 cup coconut sugar
- 1 large egg
- 2 tsp. cinnamon
- 1/4 tsp. ground cloves
- 1 tsp. baking soda
- 1 cup blanched almond flour

Cooking time - 22 minutes

Serving Size - 18

Instructions:

Whisk together the canned pumpkin, egg, coconut oil, vanilla extract, and coconut sugar till the mixture is smooth. Stir in the nutmeg, baking powder, almond flour, cinnamon, cloves, kosher salt, coconut flour, and baking soda. Continue stirring till all the ingredients blend well and form a smooth cookie dough. Fold in the chocolate chunks.

Place inside the refrigerator, covered, and chill for about an hour or so. Once the dough is ready for baking, get the oven ready by preheating it to 350 degrees F. Place 18 cookies made from the dough using an ice cream scoop on a baking sheet with parchment paper.

Let the cookies bake for about 10-12 minutes until the edges are golden and crispy.

Allow to cool for a while and then serve immediately or store for later.

9. Coconut Flour Chocolate Chip Cookies

Coconut as a substitute for refined sugar does a pretty good job when it comes to warm cookies. The texture of coconut gives a unique touch to otherwise classic cookies.

Ingredients:

- 1/3 cup sunflower seed butter or tahini
- 1 large egg
- 1/2 tsp. baking soda
- 1/3 cup coconut flour
- Flaky sea salt, for garnish
- 1/4 cup extra-virgin coconut oil
- 2/3 cup coconut sugar
- 1 tsp. vanilla extract
- 1/2 tsp. salt
- 2/3 cup chopped dark chocolate

Cooking Time - 20 minutes

Serving Size - 10

Instructions:

To 350 degrees F, get the oven preheated and get a parchment-lined cookie sheet. Whisk together the coconut sugar, sunflower seed butter, and coconut oil. Stir in the vanilla and egg; continue whisking till the mixture is smooth.

Add the coconut flour, salt, and baking soda to the mixture and continue mixing till all the ingredients are well blended. Add the chopped dark chocolate and fold it in with the mixture. Divide the dough into 10 cookies with the help of a cookie scoop.

Place the cookies on the cookie sheet and flatten a bit gently. Sprinkle flaky sea salt over the cookies. Place in the oven and bake for about 10 minutes till the cookies turn lightly browned towards the edges.

Remove from the oven once the cookies are ready. Allow to cool for a while and then either serve immediately or save for later.

10. Salted Caramel Thumbprint Cookies

Are you a caramel lover too? The same pinch, and secondly, here's my favorite, the delicious delight with caramel treat-filled in the center. You'll fall in love with this one, that's for sure.

Ingredients:

- 2 tbsp. maple syrup
- 1 and 1/4 cups blanched almond flour
- 1/4 cup coconut oil, melted
- For the caramel:
- 2 tbsp. coconut oil
- 1/2 tsp. salt
- 3 tbsp. creamy almond butter
- 2 tbsp. pure maple syrup
- For the drizzle:
- Flaky sea salt, for garnish
- 2 oz. dark chocolate, chopped

Cooking Time - 30 minutes

Serving Size - 15

Instructions:

Combine the almond flour with maple syrup and coconut oil in a mixing bowl. Form a ball out of the dough and then plastic wrap it. Chill for about an hour.

Divide the dough ball into 15 cookie balls. Press your thumb onto the middle of every cookie to form an imprint. Meanwhile, get the oven ready by preheating it to 375 degrees F.

Place all the cookies on a parchment-lined baking sheet and then place the sheet inside the oven. Bake until the cookies are about lightly browned towards the edges after ten to twelve minutes. Bring it out of the oven and gently press down the center with a small teaspoon to make space for the filling.

Prepare the caramel filling by whisking together, maple syrup with almond butter, salt, and melted coconut oil. Pour this filling into the pressed thumbprints.

Melt the chocolate in the microwave for about thirty seconds. Transfer this melted chocolate to a zip-zap bag. Drizzle this chocolate over the ready cookies. Add the finishing touch with a sprinkle of flaky sea salt.

Let the cookies get set in the refrigerator and then serve as per your liking.

11. Paleo Almond Chocolate Chunk Cookies

Sounds like some of the previous recipes, but no, it's not. As I've already said that dry fruits add a magic touch to your dishes, here's another one as proof. The nutty flavor that comes from almonds and creamy almond butter is just the best thing you can ever imagine.

Ingredients:

- 1/4 cup creamy almond butter
- 1 tsp. vanilla extract
- 1/2 tsp. salt
- 1/3 cup flaked coconut (toasted)
- 2/3 cup chopped dark chocolate
- 1/3 cup chopped almonds
- 1/2 tsp. flaky sea salt
- 1/4 cup coconut oil
- 3/4 cup coconut sugar
- 1/2 tsp. baking soda
- 1 egg
- 2 cups blanched almond flour

Cooking Time - 71 minutes

Serving Size - 14

Instructions:

Whisk the coconut sugar with the almond butter and the coconut oil in a mixing bowl till the mixture is smooth. Stir in the vanilla and egg, blend properly. Add the baking soda, salt, and almond flour to the mixture and make sure that all the ingredients are incorporated well. Fold in chopped almonds and dark chocolate.

Refrigerate the mixture fully covered for about an hour. Once the dough is ready for baking, divide it into 14 cookies with the help of a cookie scoop. Meanwhile, get the oven ready by preheating it to 350 degrees F. Place the cookies on a parchment-lined baking sheet and gently flatten each one of them. Sprinkle with the flaky sea salt and flaked coconut.

Place inside the oven and bake for about 10-12 minutes till the edges turn light brown. Once ready, bring out and allow to cool for about 5 minutes and then serve as you prefer.

12. Vegan Cranberry Orange Cookies

With the sweetness of cranberry with a tangy orange twist, this fruity cookie proves that food experiments can be crazy yet fun. Suitable for a vegan diet, this vegan cranberry-orange cookie is worth a try.

Ingredients:

- 2/3 cup coconut sugar
- 1 egg
- 1/2 tsp. baking soda
- 3/4 tsp. cinnamon
- 1 cup fresh cranberries (halved)
- 1/2 cup coconut oil
- 1 tsp. orange zest
- 1 tsp. vanilla extract
- 1/2 tsp. salt
- 2 and 1/4 cups blanched almond flour
- 1/2 cup dried cranberries

Cooking Time - 27 minutes

Serving Size - 14

Instructions:

Get the oven ready by preheating it to 350 degrees F before baking. Use parchment paper to line a baking sheet for later use.

Whisk together the orange zest, sugar, and coconut oil till the mixture is smooth. Stir in the vanilla and egg, blend well. Add the baking soda, almond flour, cinnamon, and salt to the wet mixture. Make sure that all the ingredients are mixed well. Toss the dried and fresh cranberries until they are properly folded in the mixture.

Divide the cookie dough into 14 cookies using a cookie scoop. Transfer the cookies to the parchment-lined baking sheet and flatten each of them gently. Place in the oven and bake for about twelve minutes till the center sets and the edges are somewhat golden brown.

Remove from the oven once the cookies are ready. Allow to cool for a bit and then serve or store for later, whatever you prefer.

13. Paleo Double Chocolate Cookies

We know your love for chocolate, and we know it isn't enough to just have some chocolate chips over your cookie. Hence, here is a recipe to double the chocolaty fun and give you the warm joy you have been craving for.

Ingredients:

- 3/4 cup coconut sugar
- 1 tsp. vanilla extract
- 1/2 tsp. salt
- 1 cup semi-sweet chocolate chunks
- 1/2 cup coconut oil
- 1 egg
- 1/2 tsp. baking soda
- 1 cup cocoa powder

Cooking Time - 20 minutes

Serving Size - 12

Instructions:

Get the oven ready by preheating it to 350 degrees F. Whisk together the coconut sugar and the coconut oil. Stir in the vanilla and egg; combine properly. Add the cocoa powder, salt, and baking soda. Fold in the chocolate chunks and combine the mixture well.

Divide the dough into 12 cookie balls and place them on a parchment-lined baking sheet. Let them bake for ten minutes till the cookies are properly set. Remove from the oven and let it cool down for about fifteen minutes.

Serve immediately or store in an airtight container for later.

14. Healthy Gluten-Free Chocolate Chip Cookies

Golden brown cookies with dark brown choco chips in between look so beautiful and, of course, taste so yummy too. Although it's the most classic recipe for cookies, this one is a healthy alternative for everyone, regardless of anybody's diet.

Ingredients:

- 1/3 cup coconut oil, melted
- 1 egg
- 1 and 3/4 cups almond meal
- 1/2 tsp. salt
- 1/2 cup creamy almond butter
- 1 and 1/2 cups dark chocolate chips
- 6 tbsp. maple syrup
- 2 tsp. vanilla extract
- 1/2 tsp. baking soda

Cooking Time - 15 minutes

Serving Size - 14

Instructions:

Combine the melted coconut oil, egg, almond butter, vanilla extract, and maple syrup in a medium-sized bowl till the mixture is homogeneous. Stir in the salt, baking soda, and almond meal. Toss the chocolate chips and fold them into the mixture.

Refrigerate the cookie dough for about an hour and when it is ready to bake, get the oven ready by preheating it to 350 degrees F. Divide the dough into 14 cookies with the help of a cookie scoop. Place these cookies on a baking sheet lined with parchment paper.

Bake for about ten to twelve minutes till the cookies are set, and the edges are golden brown.

Remove from the oven and allow to cool for a while. Serve warm as per your preference.

15. Chocolate Chunk Tahini Oatmeal Cookies

The strong taste of tahini and the mild bitterness of dark chocolate chunks is a great combo to try if you love unique toppings for your cookies. Try this one out and enjoy how the flavors are released slowly inside your mouth.

Ingredients:

- 1/2 cup almond flour
- 6 tbsp. maple syrup
- 1/2 tsp. salt
- 1/2 tsp. cinnamon
- 1/4 cup dark chocolate chunks
- 1 cup rolled oats, large flake
- 1/3 cup tahini

Cooking time - 20 minutes

Serving Size - 12

Instructions:

Get the oven preheated to 350 degrees F and line parchment paper on the baking sheet. Combine the cinnamon, maple syrup, and tahini till the mixture is smooth.

Stir in the oats and almond flour till properly incorporated. Fold the chocolate chunks into the mixture.

Divide the cookie dough into 12 cookies using a cookie scoop. Place the cookies on the baking sheet and press down gently. Dust some sea salt over the cookies and place them inside the oven to bake for about ten minutes.

Once the cookies are puffed and set with golden brown edges, let cool.

Serve warm and enjoy!

16. Flourless Dark Chocolate Raspberry Brownie Cookies

Berries are a fun option if you are thinking of a fruity chocolaty cookie. This raspberry dark chocolate cookie has all that you need to treat your taste buds along with being so healthy.

Ingredients:

- 1/2 cup coconut sugar
- 1/4 cup unsweetened dark cocoa powder
- 1/2 tsp. baking soda
- 1 cup dark chocolate chunks
- 1/2 cup frozen raspberries
- 3/4 cup cashew butter
- 1/4 cup maple syrup or date syrup
- 1 large egg
- 1/2 tsp. sea salt

Cooking Time - 25 minutes

Serving Size - 12

Instructions:

Get the oven preheated to 350 degrees F. Also, get the baking sheet prepared by lining it with a slip mat or parchment paper. On the other hand, in a mixing bowl, combine all the ingredients leaving the raspberries and chocolate chunks. Whisk well till all the ingredients are combined. Make sure the dough is not runny and thick enough.

Now, toss the chocolate chunks into the mixture while also adding the raspberries to it carefully, and fold them gently. Divide the cookie dough into 12 cookies and place them on the prepared baking sheet.

Place in the oven and let the cookies bake for about 11-13 minutes or until the cookies are properly set and crispy. Remove from the oven once ready and allow to cool down for about ten minutes.

Serve instantly or store for later.

17. Vegan Snowball Cookies

Snowballs aren't safe to eat, yes, they aren't, but these snowball cookies are surely the safest and tastiest thing to try. Besides, being vegan won't make you compromise your diet either. Don't they look so pretty; try and see for yourself.

Ingredients:

- 1/4 cup tapioca flour or arrowroot starch
- 1/4 tsp. sea salt
- 1 and 3/4 cups blanched almond flour
- 1/4 cup coconut sugar
- 1/3 cup finely chopped pecans
- 1/2 cup vegan butter or coconut oil
- 1 tsp. vanilla extract

For powdered sugar coating:

- 1/4 cup tapioca starch or arrowroot starch
- 1/4 cup coconut sugar

Cooking Time - 25 minutes

Serving Size - 20

Instructions:

Use a coffee grinder to mix the tapioca flour and coconut sugar into a superfine mixture for rolling the cookies after baking. Set aside. Mix the tapioca flour with the coconut oil, salt, vanilla extract, and coconut sugar in a large bowl. Stir in the pecans and almond flour till they blend well with the dough mixture.

Use a cookie scoop to form cookie balls from the dough (tablespoon size). Shape the balls into a proper round shape by rolling with your hands. Place these balls on a baking sheet lined with parchment.

Place inside the oven and bake for about ten to twelve minutes at 350 degrees F. Remove from the oven once the cookies are nicely baked, golden brown, and crispy.

Allow them to cool down for about 5 minutes. Then roll the cookies in the powdered sugar and flour mixture you prepared earlier.

Serve right away or save for later in airtight containers.

18. Paleo Cherry Almond Chocolate Chunk Cookies

One of the best options for a warm breakfast on a winter morning, these cherry almond cookies fit right beside your coffee mug.

Ingredients:

- 3/4 cup coconut sugar
- 1 tsp. vanilla extract
- 1/2 tsp. salt
- 2/3 cup chopped dark chocolate
- 1/3 cup sliced almonds (toasted)
- 1/2 cup coconut oil
- 1 egg
- 1 tsp. baking soda
- 2 1/4 cups blanched almond flour
- 1/3 cup dried unsweetened Bing cherries
- 1 cup pecans

Cooking Time - 20 minutes

Serving Size - 15

Instructions:

Get the oven preheated to 350 degrees F. In a mixing bowl, whisk the coconut sugar with the coconut oil. Stir in vanilla and the egg and mix well. Add the baking soda, salt, and almond flour to the mixture and whisk properly. Fold the cherries, chocolate, and pecans into the mixture and cover it properly using plastic wrap.

Refrigerate for about an hour and when the dough is ready for baking divide it into 15 cookies using a cookie scoop. Place them on a parchment-lined baking sheet and gently flatten each of them. Sprinkle the sliced almonds over the cookies.

Bake for about ten minutes till the edges turn golden brown and the cookies are set. Remove from the oven once ready and allow to cool down for a while.

Serve immediately, or store for whenever you prefer.

19. Gluten-Free Sourdough Chocolate Chip Cookies

Flavors of fermented sourdough mixed within the crispy crust of these fresh cookies just taste so good. Take one bite and forget everything about the workload you have pending.

Ingredients:

- 2/3 cup coconut sugar
- 1/2 cup gluten-free sourdough starter
- 1/2 tsp. baking soda
- 2 cups and 2 tbsp. blanched almond flour
- Flaky sea salt, for garnish
- 1/2 cup refined coconut oil
- 1 large egg
- 1 tsp. pure vanilla extract
- 1/2 tsp. sea salt
- 1 cup chocolate chips

Cooking Time - 21 minutes

Serving Size - 12

Instructions:

Whisk the coconut oil with coconut sugar. Stir in the sourdough starter, vanilla, and egg; mix well till the mixture is smooth. Add the baking soda, salt, and almond flour to the mixture, and make sure all the ingredients are incorporated well. Toss the chocolate chips and fold them into the mixture.

Plastic wraps the dough and place it in the refrigerator to chill for about an hour. When the dough is ready for baking, divide the dough into 12 cookies using a cookie scoop.

Place the cookies on a baking sheet lined with parchment paper and flatten gently and dust the flaky salt over the cookies. Meanwhile, get the oven preheated to 350 degrees F.

Place in the oven and bake for ten minutes until the edges begin to turn golden brown.

Remove the dough from the oven once the cookies are properly set, and then allow it to cool for a bit.

Serve immediately or save for later in airtight containers.

20. Almond Blueberry Breakfast Cookies

As the name itself suggests, these cookies fit best at the breakfast table. So why don't you go fetch some fresh blueberries from the garden and bake some as a surprise for tomorrow's breakfast?

Ingredients:

- 1/2 cup creamy almond butter
- 1 egg
- 1 cup blanched almond flour
- 1 tsp. baking soda
- 3/4 cup fresh blueberries
- 1/4 cup and 2 tbsp. coconut oil
- 1/2 cup coconut sugar
- 1 tsp. vanilla extract
- 1/2 cup gluten-free rolled oats
- 1/2 tsp. kosher salt
- 1/2 cup almonds, chopped and toasted

Cooking Time - 25 minutes

Serving Size - 16

Instructions:

Get the oven preheated to 350 degrees F. Also, prepare a baking sheet by using parchment paper to line it. On the other hand, prepare the dough by first mixing the coconut sugar with the almond butter and coconut oil. Stir in the vanilla and egg and continue mixing till the mixture is smooth.

Add the rolled oats, salt, almond flour, and baking soda to the mixture and combine. Toss the blueberries and toasted almonds till they just fold into the dough. Cover and chill for about an hour.

Divide the dough to form 12 cookies using a cookie scoop. Place these cookies on the prepared baking sheet and press down all of them gently. Place in the oven and bake for about ten minutes till the cookies turn crispy and lightly browned.

Remove from the oven once the cookies are set and allow to cool down. Serve as per your preference.

21. Vegan Jam Thumbprint Cookies

Bread and jam surely go so well with each other, but the cookie jam combo isn't any less than that. This recipe here will prove to you in case you have any doubts.

Ingredients:

- 1/4 cup coconut oil, melted
- 1/2 tsp. salt
- 1 and 1/4 cups blanched almond flour
- 1/4 cup refined sugar-free fruit jam
- 3 tbsp. maple syrup

Cooking Time - 25 minutes

Serving Size - 15

Instructions:

In a large mixing bowl, add all the ingredients leaving the jam and whisk well. Shape the dough into a ball and then use plastic wrap to cover it adequately. Chill in the refrigerator for about an hour till the dough is ready for baking.

Prepare the oven to be preheated to 375 degrees F. Use parchment paper to line a baking sheet. Take the dough out of the refrigerator and divide it to form 15 balls.

Press down the balls onto the baking sheet making an imprint in the middle of the cookies. Fill the imprints with the jam and then transfer the sheet to the oven.

Bake for about ten minutes till the cookies get set, and the edges turn golden brown. Take them out of the oven once the cookies are ready and leave them on a tray to cool down for a while.

Serve right away or store in airtight containers for later.

22. Cashew Butter Cookies

The nutty flavor of cashew nuts with creamy butter essence mixed within the insides of these crispy delights works magic in your mouth. Have a mouthful of this one while thinking if I'm right or wrong.

Ingredients:

- 1/4 cup maple syrup
- 1/4 tsp. salt
- 1 cup creamy cashew butter
- 1/4 cup ground flax seed

Cooking Time - 25 minutes

Serving Size - 20

Instructions:

Add the cashew butter, salt, flaxseed, and maple syrup to a large mixing bowl. Combine till the mixture is creamy and smooth.

Prepare the oven by preheating it to 350 degrees F.

Form balls out of the cookie mixture and place the balls on a baking sheet that isn't greased.

Bake for about 17 minutes till the cookies get set properly. Transfer to a tray and allow to cool down.

Serve right away or save for later in airtight containers.

23. Sugar-Free Carrot Cake Oatmeal Cookies

Why limit the use of carrots in main course meals when it makes such delicious desserts. The cookies taste so amazingly sweet even without any sugar by the grace of carrots.

Ingredients:

- 3/4 cup gluten-free flour or whole wheat
- 1 and 1/2 tsp. ground cinnamon
- 1/4 tsp. salt
- 1 large egg white
- 1/4 cup maple syrup
- 3/4 cup carrot, freshly grated
- 1 cup instant oats
- 1 and 1/2 tsp. baking powder
- 1/4 tsp. ground nutmeg
- 2 tbsp. coconut oil
- 1 tsp. vanilla extract
- 5 tbsp. nonfat milk

Cooking Time - 30 minutes

Serving Size - 15

Instructions:

Combine the flour, cinnamon, salt, oats, and nutmeg in a large mixing bowl. In another bowl, mix the vanilla, egg white, baking powder, and coconut oil. Add the milk and maple syrup and stir.

Add the flour mixture to the egg white mixture and stir whisk properly till the ingredients are incorporated. Toss the carrots in and fold them into the mixture. Cover with plastic wrap and refrigerate for about an hour.

Get the oven ready by preheating it to 325 degrees F. Also, use parchment paper to line the baking sheet. Once the dough is ready for baking, divide it into 15 balls using a cookie scoop. Press down gently onto the baking sheet.

Bake for about 11-12 minutes till the cookies get set and the edges look crispy. Remove from the oven once ready and allow to cool down.

Serve immediately or store in airtight containers.

24. Sugar-Free Cream Cheese Cookies

Cream Cheese cannot stay out of the options when speaking about breakfast desserts. One of the lightest foods with the heaviest impact on your sense of taste, these cream cheese cookies will leave your mind baffled.

Ingredients:

- 2 oz. cream cheese
- 1 large egg
- 1/4 tsp. sea salt
- 3 cups wholesome yum blanched almond flour
- 1/4 cup unsalted butter
- 1/3 cup best monk fruit allulose blend
- 2 tsp. vanilla extract
- 1 tbsp. sour cream

Cooking Time - 25 minutes

Serving Size - 24

Instructions:

Prepare the oven by preheating it to 350 degrees F. Also, use parchment paper to line a baking sheet.

In a large mixing bowl, whisk together the sweetener, cream cheese, and butter till the mixture is smooth and creamy. Stir in the egg, salt, vanilla, and sour cream; whisk properly till incorporated.

Add the almond flour half cup at a time while beating continuously to form the cookie dough. Once ready, divide the dough into 24 cookies with the help of a cookie scoop. Place the cookies on the prepared sheet and then press down gently with a spatula.

Bake for about fifteen minutes till the cookies are golden brown and crispy enough. Remove from the oven and let them cool down for a while.

Serve right away or store in airtight containers.

25. Flavored Meringue Cookies

With the sweetness of sugar substituted by meringue, these cookies are a great option if you happen to have a sweet tooth.

Ingredients:

- 1 cup granulated sugar substitute, no-calorie
- 1/4 tsp. cream of tartar
- 1 and 1/2 tsp. strawberry Jell-O mix, sugar-free
- 1/4 tsp. salt
- 6 egg whites, room temperature

Cooking Time - 2 hours 15 minutes

Serving Size - 24

Instructions:

Prepare the oven by preheating it to 250 degrees F. Also, use parchment paper for lining two baking sheets.

Beat the sugar with the gelatin mix in a small-sized bowl. In a separate mixing bowl, whisk the cream with the egg whites and salt till the mixture forms coarse peaks. While whisking, keep stirring in the gelatin mix 1 tbsp. at a time.

Prepare a plastic bag for squeezing the dough into the baking sheets by cutting 1/4 in. off a resealable gallon-size plastic bag corner. Shove a large cake decorating tip towards the opening of the bag for a decorative effect on the cookies. Make sure the tip fits tight.

Fill the plastic bag with the cookie mixture and form 1 tbsp. sized dollops onto the baking sheets. Design however you wish.

Place in the oven and bake for about one hour and thirty minutes until the cookies look set and crisp. Once the cookies are ready, take them out of the oven and allow them to cool down for a while.

Serve immediately or save for later.

26. Sugar-Free Date Cookies

How can we forget about dates when speaking about dry fruits? Substitute for sugar, the sweetness of dates works pretty fine on cookies.

Ingredients:

- 1/4 cup chopped pecans
- 1/2 very ripe banana, mashed
- 2 tbsp. butter, melted
- 1 cup all-purpose flour
- 1 tsp. cinnamon
- 1 cup chopped dates
- 1 tsp. salt
- 1/4 cup water
- 1 large egg, lightly beaten
- 1/2 tsp. vanilla extract
- 1 tsp. baking powder

Cooking Time - 30 minutes

Serving Size - 18

Instructions:

Prepare the oven by preheating it to 350 degrees F. Also, use parchment paper for lining a baking sheet for later use.

In a large mixing bowl, add the pecans, banana, butter, dates, vanilla, egg, and water; combine well.

In another bowl, beat the baking powder, cinnamon, flour, and salt. Add the date mixture to this mixture and stir till a combined dough is formed.

Use a cookie scoop to press scoops of the cookie dough onto the prepared sheet. Flatten gently with a spatula. Transfer the sheet to the oven and bake for about 10-12 minutes till the cookies get set and golden brown.

Once ready, take them out of the oven and let them cool down for a while.

Serve immediately or store in airtight containers.

27. Almond Crescent Cookies

Cute-looking cookies will surely be the kid's next favorite dessert. These almond crescent cookies contain taste and health content in equal amounts.

Ingredients:

- 3 and 3/4 cups almond flour
- 1 and 1/4 cups granulated sweetener, low-carb
- 1 and 1/2 tsp. almond extract
- 1/4 tsp. salt
- 1 tsp. powdered sweetener, for topping
- 1 cup butter
- 1/2 cup coconut flour
- 1 tsp. vanilla extract
- 1 cup sliced almonds, for coating

Cooking Time - 40 minutes

Serving Size - 24

Instructions:

Prepare the oven by preheating it to 350 degrees F. On the other hand, beat the sweetener with salt and butter in a small bowl. Stir in the vanilla and almond extracts. Eventually, add all the remaining ingredients except the ones for the topping i.e., sliced almonds and powdered sweetener.

Whisk the mixture until smooth and form 3 in. long logs out of the dough. Take the almond slices in a bowl in which you have to roll the logs. Form crescent-shaped cookies out of the logs and place them on a parchment-lined baking sheet.

Place in the oven and bake for about 11-14 minutes till the cookies are set. Remove them from the oven and let them cool down.

Once ready, dust powdered sweeteners over them, serve them right away, or store them in airtight containers.

28. Keto Breakfast Cookies

Besides a glass of warm milk, warm cookies are the perfect option to brighten up your boring keto diet.

Ingredients:

- 2 tbsp. coconut flour
- 2/3 cup granular sweetener
- 1 tsp. vanilla
- 1/2 tsp. kosher salt
- 1/2 cup hemp hearts
- 1 and 1/2 cups almond flour
- 1/2 cup melted butter
- 2 large eggs
- 1 tsp. baking powder
- 1/2 cup sliced almonds

Cooking Time - 23 minutes

Serving Size - 16

Instructions:

Prepare the oven by preheating it to 350 degrees F. Also, use parchment for lining a baking sheet to be used later.

Add all the ingredients to a large mixing bowl and whisk till the mixture forms a smooth cookie dough.

Use a cookie scoop to form 16 cookies out of the dough mixture. Place these cookies on the prepared baking sheet. Press down gently to flatten.

Bake for about 12 minutes till the edges begin turning golden brown. Remove from the oven once the cookies seem ready and let them cool down for a while.

Serve immediately after that or save for later in airtight containers.

29. Sugar-Free Keto Coconut Macaroons

Not exactly that crispy cookie, but somewhat like it, these coconut macaroons are the best dessert option if looking for something to impress somebody.

Ingredients:

- 3/4 cup sugar substitute, low-carb
- 3/4 tsp. sugar-free vanilla extract
- 3-4 cups unsweetened shredded coconut
- 2 large eggs
- 2 cups sugar-free chocolate chips
- 1/3 cup water
- 1/4 tsp. sea salt

Cooking Time - 22 minutes

Serving Size - 20

Instructions:

Get the oven ready by, preheating it to 350 degrees F. Also, prepare a baking sheet by spraying non-stick spray over it.

In a medium-sized saucepan, mix the low-carb sweetener, vanilla extract, salt, and water; allow to come to a boil while stirring over moderate heat. Remove from heat.

Add the coconut flakes and egg to a food blender, pour the boiled mixture, and pulse to prepare the cookie dough. Divide the dough into cookie mounds using a cookie scoop. Place the mounds on the prepared baking sheet.

Place the baking sheet inside the oven and bake for about eight minutes, then turn the pan to the other side. Let it bake for 4 more minutes till the edges of the cookies become golden brown. Meanwhile, melt the chocolate chips in a microwave-safe bowl inside the microwave for about 4-5 minutes.

Remove from the oven and let cool down. Once ready, drizzle melted chocolate over them and enjoy!

30. Low-Carb Holiday Cookies

Holidays are great when you have the right food to accompany you. These low-carb holiday cookies are a great option for a little treat with the amazing frosting it has.

Ingredients:

For the cookies:

- 1 cup almond flour
- 1/2 cup ricotta
- 1/2 tsp. baking powder
- 2 eggs
- 1/4 tsp. salt
- 1/2 cup Lakanto
- 1/4 cup unsweetened cocoa powder

For the frosting:

- 4 oz. cream cheese softened
- 1/4 tsp. extract, e.g.- almond, peppermint, optional
- 1/4 cup heavy cream
- 1 tsp. low carb sprinkles
- 2 tbsp. confectioners' swerve

Cooking Time - 22 minutes

Serving Size - 12

Instructions:

Get the oven ready by preheating it to 350 degrees F. Whisk the egg in a mixing bowl till stiff peaks arise. Stir in the remaining ingredients and continue whisking till the mixture is smooth.

Prepare a baking sheet with parchment paper for lining it. Use a cookie scoop to scoop out 12 cookies onto the baking sheet and press down a little.

Transfer to the oven and bake for about 11-13 minutes or until the cookies get set and turn golden brown around the edges.

Remove from the oven and allow to cool. Meanwhile, prepare the frosting by tossing all the frosting ingredients into a food processor; process till the mixture is creamy and smooth.

Use a piping bag to frost the cookies evenly. Add the finishing touch with the sprinkles and serve!

Conclusion

With this recipe, we have come to the end of our cookbook, and I hope that all the recipes will be more than enough to satisfy your sweet tooth. Each one has its uniqueness in all aspects, be it taste, aroma or looks. Moreover, every recipe is favorable for all sorts of diets, and the plus point is that you don't have to compromise with your taste buds. Make sure you try each of them to determine which one to choose or a favorite. Believe me, it's going to be a really hard choice as all of them are just so amazingly exquisite.

So, even if you aren't yet convinced that these are indeed the finest recipes for healthy cookies, it's time to try them for yourself. Put on your mittens and get ready with your baking gears, for it's a cookie challenge!

Epilogues

There are days I feel like quitting, but then I remember readers like you, and my heart swells with pride at the love you show me by buying each and every book I put out there.

I am delighted, to say the least, to know that people like you take their time to download, read and cook with my books!

Thank you so much for accepting me and all that I have shared with the world.

While I am basking in the euphoria of your love and commitment to my books, I would beseech you to kindly drop your reviews and feedback. I would love to read from you!

Head to Amazon.com to drop your reviews!!!

Thank you

Charlotte Long

About the Author

For the past 10 years, Charlotte has been collating and exploring different dishes from different cultures of the world. Birthed and raised in Ohio, Charlotte grew up to know that cooking is a magical activity that requires a certain degree of commitment and love to be carried out.

She learnt this from her grandmother who was one of the best local chefs in Ohio then. Charlotte's grandmother would always create and invent new recipes and also refurbish old ones. The result of it is her passion for cooking cum a large book of special recipes that Charlotte inherited.

Using her grandmother's recipe book as her foundational training guide, Charlotte wore her grandmother's chef shoes to become one of the best chefs in Ohio and its environment.

Charlotte has written different recipe books, and she is currently touring the Caribbean and looking for new recipes to unravel.

Printed in Great Britain
by Amazon

42541686R00051